a pocket RHYME
Imagination for a new generation

2006 Poetry Competition for 7-11 year-olds

YoungWriters

Verses From Yorkshire
Edited by Heather Killingray

YoungWriters

First published in Great Britain in 2007 by:
Young Writers
Remus House
Coltsfoot Drive
Peterborough
PE2 9JX
Telephone: 01733 890066
Website: www.youngwriters.co.uk

All Rights Reserved

© Copyright Contributors 2007

SB ISBN 978-1 84602 777 2

Foreword

Young Writers was established in 1991 and has been passionately devoted to the promotion of reading and writing in children and young adults ever since. The quest continues today. Young Writers remains as committed to the nurturing of poetic and literary talent as ever.

This year's Young Writers competition has proven as vibrant and dynamic as ever and we are delighted to present a showcase of the best poetry from across the UK and in some cases overseas. Each poem has been selected from a wealth of *A Pocketful Of Rhyme* entries before ultimately being published in this, our fourteenth primary school poetry series.

Once again, we have been supremely impressed by the overall quality of the entries we have received. The imagination, energy and creativity which has gone into each young writer's entry made choosing the poems a challenging and often difficult but ultimately hugely rewarding task - the general high standard of the work submitted ensured this opportunity to bring their poetry to a larger appreciative audience.

We sincerely hope you are pleased with this final collection and that you will enjoy *A Pocketful Of Rhyme Verses From Yorkshire* for many years to come.

Contents

Castle Hills Primary School
    Oliver Green (10)   1
    Katie Rowe (10)   1
    John Gray (10)   2
    Elizabeth Deere (10)   2
    Joshua Bertman (11)   3
    Alicia Hamilton (10)   3
    Hannah Mycock (10)   4
    Michael Church (10)   4
    Bradley Williamson (11)   4

Cullingworth Village Primary School
    George Halliwell (9)   5
    Holly Thelwell (9)   5
    Bethany Lomas (9)   6
    Sophie Fardy (8)   6
    Luca Zenti (8)   7
    Joshua Finch (9)   7
    Jacob Wood (9)   7
    Edward Hodgson (8)   8
    Katie Handford (8)   8
    Georgia Beith (8)   9
    Joe Ogden (8)   9
    Max Blair (9)   10
    Andrew Roberts (8)   10
    Adam Vaux (9)   11
    Liam Mayling (8)   11
    James Fardy (10)   12
    Levi Hanson (11)   12
    Emily Hodgson (10)   13
    Sophia Daramy-Williams (9)   13
    Amna Ali (8)   14
    Amy Hanson (9)   14
    Abigail Whitehouse (8)   14
    Olivia Dalton (8)   15
    Charis Halliwell (8)   15
    Holly Robinson (7)   15
    Lucy Riley (8)   16
    Francesca Haigh (7)   16

Tasha Smith (8)	16
Lauren Hawkes (7)	17
Rhianna Lavery (8)	17
Eve Knowles (7)	17
Joshua Hardy (10)	18
Holly Spence (10)	18
Alex Wright (10)	19
Sarah Bell (11)	19
Conor Mayling (11)	19
Jenny Makinson (10)	20
Max Milne (8)	20
Julia Proctor (9)	21
Lewis Whitehouse (8)	21
Rosie Findlay (8)	22
Matthew Wiggins (8)	22
Aimee Robinson (8)	22
Samantha Grimshaw (7)	23
Georgina Dawson (7)	23
Callum Whitehouse (8)	23
Sam Clare (10)	24
Jack Griggs (8)	24
Joe Williams (8)	24
Tom Williams (9)	25
Joe Robinson (10)	25
Harrison Bailey (10)	25
Sam Ellis (10)	26
Henry Presland (10)	26
Paul Norfolk (10)	27
Sally Handford (10)	27
Ellie Holgate (10)	27
Joe Perrin (10)	28
Alicia Brigg (10)	28
Joe Ferguson (10)	29
Leah Kerr (10)	29
Molly Harrison (10)	30
William Keeley (9)	30
Luke Crowther (9)	31
George Trudgill (10)	31
Jenny Riley (9)	32
Jessica Cain (9)	32
Daniel Ogden (10)	33

Samantha Robinson (9)	33
Freya George (10)	33

Dalton Listerdale J&I School

Edward Donaldson (8)	33
Bradley Smith (8)	34
Jessica Taylor (8)	34
Nula Fell-Andrews (8)	34
Thomas Worrall (8)	34
Nicola Beaumont (8)	35
Lauren Carr (8)	35
Sadie Agana (8)	35
Emma Botfield (8)	35
Ryan Bagnall (8)	36
Ashley Wilson (8)	36
Oliver Curran (9)	36
Benjamin Malin (8)	36
Lucia Del Pozo-Largo (8)	37

Dodworth St John The Baptist CE (VA) Primary School

Harris Moran (9)	37
Madigan Patzelt (9)	37
Sheldon Delices (8)	38
Emma Martin (8)	39
Hannah Carr (9)	39
Tomas Sellars (8)	40
Adelle Wragg (8)	40
Imogen Wainwright (8)	40
Ashley Horsfield (9)	41

Field Lane JI&N School

Naeema Goolab & Saira Mahmood (10)	41
Hamzah Laher (10)	42
Aysha Hussain (10)	42
Muhammed Talkeen Pandor (11)	43
Samee Masood (10)	43
Tayyub Hussain (10)	44
Aamirah Sidat (10)	44
Naafiah Loonat, Haarla Sadiq & Ammaarah Pandor (10)	45
Mehran Ishaq (10)	45

Garton-on-the-Wolds CE (VC) Primary School
Lizzy Purdy (11)	46
Johnny Wheatley (10)	46
Abigail Longney (9)	47
Emily Iveson, Eleanor Lodge & Danielle Wheatley (8)	47
James Watts (9)	48
Chris Fearnley (9)	48
Oliver Noblett (10)	49
Matthew Evans (9)	49
Tom Iveson (10)	50
Josh Young & Jake Bowers (9)	50
Harvey Booth (11)	51

Meadstead Primary School
Victoria Cox (8)	51
Andrew Jessop (9)	52
Patrick Dexter (8)	52
Helena Quinn (9)	53
Chelsea Levitt (8)	53
Ethan King (8)	54

Melbourne Community Primary School
Lara Wilson (11)	54
Edward Wilkinson (11) & Matty Jackson (10)	55
Molly Hogan (11) & Megan Lund (10)	56
Declan Freeman (9)	57

Rawmarsh Monkwood Junior School
Megan Wright (8)	57
Michaela Richardson (8)	57
Megan Scott & Alice Bragg (8)	58
Isobel Gough & Carly Jones (8)	59
Bradley Hammond & Connor Spyve (8)	59
Anna Rodgers (8)	59
Elisha Ingleby (8)	60
Claire Hobson & Bethany Hague (8)	60
Liam Larkin & Alex Fields (8)	61
Lisa Kelsall & Dylan Robinson (8)	61

St Andrew's CE Primary School, Hull

Calum Ward (9)	62
Courtney Clark (8)	63
Jay Farrow (8)	63
Jadzia Johnson (8)	64
Banu Senol (8)	64
Rachel Smith (9)	65
Luke Brady (8)	65
Natasha Barker (8)	66
Rhys King (8)	66
Shanice Michaels (9)	67
Sam Stevenson (8)	68

St Mary's CE Primary School, Wetherby

Megan Murphy (8)	68
Alice Whitelam (8)	69
Ruby Barrett (8)	69
Roxanne Frost (10)	69

St Thomas More Primary School, Sheffield

Barnaby Peech (9)	70
Jade Fletcher (10)	70
Olivia Lomas (8)	71
Charlotte Betts (8)	71
Grant Williams (9)	72
Frances Hemingway (8)	72
Lauren Hodkin (10)	73
Natasha Doyle (9)	73
Kayleigh Evelyn (9)	74
Bethany Smedley (8)	74
Lauren Raynor-Bennett (9)	75
Hannah Stocks (9)	75
Brendan Maycock (8)	76
Alex Radford (9)	76
Grace Swift (9)	77
Briony Colton (9)	77
Levi Brock (8)	78
Joe Talbot (9)	78
Paris Thorpe (9)	79
James Killeen (8)	79
Hollie Roberts (8)	80

Catherine Dwaine (8)   80
Adam Cohen (9)   81
Olivia Nicholson (9)   81

Serlby Park School
Rebecca White (10)   82
Daniel Hawley (11)   82
Kimberley Smith (10)   82
Sophie Cave (10)   83
Eily Wilson (11)   83
Makenzie Tomlinson (10)   83
Kelly Smith (10)   84
Dale Sawyer (10)   84
Ryan Day (10)   84
Jake Renshaw (11)   85
Shannon O'Hara (10)   85
Amy Ellis & Chloe Lukey (10)   85
Tia Morris (7)   86
Paige O'Keeffe (7)   86
Connor McGowan (10)   86
Jasmine Spowart (10)   87
Chelsea Peace (10)   87
Glenn Malkin (11), Jeren Bridgett & Devon Brammer (10)   87
Luke Butters & Lewis Coxon (10)   88
Charlie Arnott (10)   88
Emma Hay (10) & Sarah Taylor (11)   88
Robyn Hanley (10)   89

Treeton CE Primary School
Megan Wilson (10)   89
Josh Pierpoint (10)   90
Adam Walton (10)   90
Bethany Farmer (10)   91
Natalie Shawcroft (10)   91
Amy Burton (10)   92
Mica Leaning (10)   92
Matthew Badger (10)   93

The Poems

Rock Pools

Rock pools sit, shimmering in the sand,
Crabs snap their claws in the wet water.
Limpets suck, as the waves crash against them.
Fish paddle into the dark.

Barnacles cling onto the rugged rocks.
Hermit crabs scuttle into the mysterious unknown.
Razor shells bury themselves into the sand.
Sea snails curl themselves up into their hard shells.

Icy cold rock pool
Silent in the night.
The animals are sleeping,
For the next day awaits.

Oliver Green (10)
Castle Hills Primary School

The Beach

I hear the seagulls crying.
I see a crab scuttling under a rock.
The water is glimmering in the rock pools,
Sea anemones cling to the rocks.
Green and brown seaweed floats in the water,
Fish dart by.

The sand glows in the sun,
I hear a pebble splash into the water.
Shells crunch under my feet,
The wind blows ripples across the water,
I see reflections in its surface.
The tide is coming in.

Katie Rowe (10)
Castle Hills Primary School

The Beach

The beach is sandy,
The sea is wet.
Rock pools infested,
With scuttling crabs.

When the tide is out,
You can walk for miles.
When the tide is in,
You can't.

The waves crash,
Sending fish flying,
Over to,
The other side.

John Gray (10)
Castle Hills Primary School

Rock Pool

The ancient rock pool waits silently.
Crabs scuttle on the rocky bottom.
Anemones stick to the rugged rocks.
Slippery seaweed on the still rocks.
Hermit crabs slowly emerging from their shells.
Seagulls screeching high above.
Rocks wait quiet and silently,
Sea snails like to be quiet and motionless.
Then all is calm.

Elizabeth Deere (10)
Castle Hills Primary School

Rock Pool

Rock pools have so much nature.
Crabs snapping at fish.
Fishes running from crabs.
Limpets sticking to rugged rocks.
Hermit crabs emerge after their sleep.
Seaweed hides crabs.
Fossils hide in their home.
Anemones waving their colourful tentacles.
Starfish stick there silently.
Here comes the waves.
All creatures hide and wait for the tide.

Joshua Bertman (11)
Castle Hills Primary School

Rock Pools

Crabs hide behind seaweed,
Starfishes sit on the ground,
Limpets suck onto rocks,
Crabs swim about.

The shimmering waters shine in the sun,
Pebbles fall into the rock pools,
Sea snails sit at the bottom of the water.

Everything starts to calm down.
The children have gone.
The creatures are ready to go to sleep.

Alicia Hamilton (10)
Castle Hills Primary School

Rock Pools

The rock pools sit on the seabed,
Hermit crabs emerge from out of their shells.
Star fishes wait for their prey,
Pebbles settle on the orange sand.
Crabs move this way and that,
They settle into their home.
Rocks form into a circle.
Sea snails suck onto rugged rocks like glue.
Everything is quiet until morning starts.

Hannah Mycock (10)
Castle Hills Primary School

Rock Pools

Rock pools; quiet animals silently moving around.
Silently, hermit crabs emerge from their shells.
Creatures scuttling on the sand.
Limpets stick to the rocks like glue.
Barnacles are really small.
Different kinds of shells in the rock pools.
The seagulls land and try to catch animals.
It's very exciting seeing prawns speed off.

Michael Church (10)
Castle Hills Primary School

Rock Pools

Hermit crabs emerge from their shells.
Fishes darting through the icy cold waters.
Rock pool waters shimmering.
Crabs scuttling under rugged rocks.
Anemones shaking their fragile tentacles.
Sea horses swimming in the shallows.

Bradley Williamson (11)
Castle Hills Primary School

A Speedy Cheetah

Fast and elegant
Running for joy
Killing its prey
Think it's a toy

Its hind legs delicate maybe
Like furry heads with Chinese whiskers
Gazelles act like babies
Mostly little cheeky misters

Hippo, crocodile, wildebeest, buffalo
And little swallow
Lion, tiger, leopard
A little tiny shepherd
Hyena, wild dog are like each other
But most of all I like that cheetah!

George Halliwell (9)
Cullingworth Village Primary School

New York

I can see the people driving fast cars,
In jail there are terrorists behind bars.

Outside guarding, were confused cops,
Villains sneaking around in shops.
There are lots of sights to see,
Cold rain weather, trickling down my knee,
Lots of people walking around,
Lots of people chattering and making a sound.

People eating delicious food,
Now I'm in New York, I'm in a good mood!

Yummy smells blowing everywhere,
I now regret looking on the map and shrieking,
'I'm not going there!'

Holly Thelwell (9)
Cullingworth Village Primary School

Hong Kong

I took a flight to colourful Hong Kong
The plane flight was boring, it took so long.
When I got there my dreams flew away
When I thought what it would look like in Hong Kong today.

I asked somebody where my hotel was
But all he said was, 'Ching chong,' cos
Finally I found my way
Then I said to myself, 'Finally sometime today.'

In the morning I went outside
Then I watched a parade march past with pride
It was very colourful and very bright
But when the lions came past, I was full of fright.

In the middle of the day it was boiling
And the food started spoiling
I had some food in the neighbourhood
And all I can say is, 'It tasted good.'

The people are all so nice in the city
All the girls' dresses are very pretty
Everybody said, 'I'm still not there'
But I'm in Hong Kong now I swear.

Bethany Lomas (9)
Cullingworth Village Primary School

In Venice

When I got off the boat,
I saw the lovely buildings of Venice surrounding me.
Then the delicious lip smacking smell of cheesy pizza and pasta.
Also the smell of salty sea air, is hanging about.
There are some creepy crawlies in the trees.
Now some spiders are crawling about.
I can now see some little people with black hair walking about.

Sophie Fardy (8)
Cullingworth Village Primary School

Venice

My dream had come true
When I stepped foot in Venice
That was the day I met Auntie Fennis.
Then I left her alone in her little old home
To check out the rest of this marvellous place.
I went to the bar to check out the streets
But when I got there, not a single car!
Instead of cars there were some boats,
Instead of streets there was just some water.
Rich, chubby people cracking the moats.
Fish splattering all about,
Then the barman told me to get out.
And that was the end of my trip to Venice.

Luca Zenti (8)
Cullingworth Village Primary School

George's Jam

George's jam went *bang!*
When his big brother went *boo!*
The jam was all over the floor.
The cat came in and licked all the jam off the floor
Mum came in and said, 'You silly boy! Get to bed now.'
And that's what happened to George's Jam.

Joshua Finch (9)
Cullingworth Village Primary School

Rollerblading

Rollerblading is fun
Especially when you go fast
But not too fast
Or you might crash into a wall
. . . or a prickly bush.

Jacob Wood (9)
Cullingworth Village Primary School

Bombay

I took a plane to beautiful Bombay
And it took all evening and all day.
When I was there, I looked around
And there was a smell of delicious, tasty wonderful food.

There were elephants and cows
Dressed up in bells and capes.
All the people were kind,
And they kept admiring their wonderful minds.

The colours on the people were bright and brown.
The ladies were dressed up in saris all sparkling around them.
All the palaces were beautiful and gold
And you could hardly stop admiring them.
The tigers were waiting for some delicious food,
The very tall grass.
There were festivals and weddings going all day.
The sun was so warm, you could see the
Glittering bright fading away.
But then I went back from beautiful Bombay.

Edward Hodgson (8)
Cullingworth Village Primary School

Imagining

I have always imagined going to Singapore.
But I have never been there before.
I imagined the white waves crashing against the shore
And on the streets there wouldn't even be an apple core.
I imagined the smell of spicy curries and the saltiest fish
                                        you've ever smelt
And the taste of ice cream that never melts.
I imagined people dressed up in colourful clothes
And in the golden wondrous temples lots of shows.
I imagined big harbours and big boats
And near the harbour one big moat.
And now I have been, it was much better than I imagined.

Katie Handford (8)
Cullingworth Village Primary School

My Trip To China

On my trip to China,
I went to a beautiful diner.
The smells were beautiful but the food looked even better,
I had some food but all I can say is it tasted lovely.

When I got out the sky was blue,
When I looked at the animals it was a zoo.
When I got to the main street I could hear the sound of feet,
Then a big, beautiful temple came into view
I sat upon a little seat.

But now I might meet some people they look very kind,
They showed me the whole of China, I hope they didn't mind.
All the smells I could smell they were lip-smacking,
Now I really have to go, it was time I was packing.

I had a great time in China
But that is all I did.

Georgia Beith (8)
Cullingworth Village Primary School

Nice

I took a train to Nice under the sea, in the Channel Tunnel,
It was very dark.

When I got there I could smell the plain food,
It did smell nice,
When I tasted some food it was very spicy.

There are checked dresses and red trousers
White, black, orange, green and yellow T-shirts very colourful.

The buildings are grand but big and short,
Poor people's houses are tatty and thin but high.
Young people are skinny and short
But the old people are as big as giants and very wrinkly.

Joe Ogden (8)
Cullingworth Village Primary School

Madrid

When I went to Madrid
I ate a big squid
Chopped up with garlic and then deep fried,
The smell was so strong
I almost cried.
The church bells were ringing
The choir was singing
On the wall of the church
Something scurried by
It was a dotty lizard
Hard to see in the strong sun blizzard
The swooping swallows dance in the sky
I can hardly see them, they fly so high.
Goodbye Madrid I had a lot of fun
I enjoyed the food and the sun.

Max Blair (9)
Cullingworth Village Primary School

A Poem About Palma

I flew to Palma last week,
The landscape is definitely not bleak.
The houses are white, and very bright.
The beaches are very hot and golden,
Look at the ships in the docks!
All the people buying things in the fashionable shops,
The clipperty clop of the horse and carriage.
The palm trees are swaying gently
The smell of coffee from the coffee shops
The smell of fish from the harbour
The smell of fish on the pan.
And that was the end of my holiday in Palma.

Andrew Roberts (8)
Cullingworth Village Primary School

In Madrid

I went to Madrid and met a friend called Sid
The beaches were glistening in the sunlight
In the plane it was an amazing height
I was scared of fright.

When they speak it sounds like singing
Because it sounds so deafening
In the shop there are loads of sweets
And in the café there are so many seats
You can't even see.
There are loads of people who sound suspicious
Whilst I am eating curry that's delicious.

When the fish is in my mouth
It tastes like it comes from the south
The weather is so very hot
It made me break a precious pot.

When we were coming home
We suddenly saw a flying gnome
When we were coming back in the car
We thought Madrid was so far.

Adam Vaux (9)
Cullingworth Village Primary School

New York

I got the plane to New York
When I got off I saw a crowded place.
There were shops everywhere
Shops outside.
Smells like food and pigeons
There were
Trams taking people to places.
Enormous skyscrapers everywhere.
I asked for a yellow taxi to take me to a hotel.

Liam Mayling (8)
Cullingworth Village Primary School

Cardboard

I'm the king,
I'm the Lord,
I'm cardboard!

You can bend me,
You can squish me,
You can cut me,
You can stick me.

I own a Ford
'Cause I'm the Lord,
It's down the road,
It carries a load.

I'm brilliant,
I'm cool,
I'm not a fool!

I'm card, card,
Cardboard!

James Fardy (10)
Cullingworth Village Primary School

Dog

Fast sprinter,
Paw printer,
Paw pacer,
Cat chaser,
Wind blaster,
Bone master,
Deafening barker,
Nosy parker,
Protective pooch,
Always mooch,
Day snoozer,
Food lover.

Levi Hanson (11)
Cullingworth Village Primary School

The House Next Door

It's the house next door,
It's dark,
It's spooky,
It's creaky,
It's dull.
Why does it live near me?

There are monsters,
There are bats,
There are ghosts,
There are rats,
Why does it live near me?

Last night,
I was cuddling Ted,
When I saw someone dead!
Why does it live near me?
That's the house next door.

Emily Hodgson (10)
Cullingworth Village Primary School

Korea

Walking just walking down the
Capital city of Korea,
You'd see black cars mainly zooming
Down the road.

Driving in the countryside you'd see
Beautiful mountains on
The side, with wonderful plants
Growing nicely.

I couldn't oh, couldn't help smelling
That wonderful food of theirs.

Who really wouldn't go to this
Wonderful, wonderful place of Seoul.

Sophia Daramy-Williams (9)
Cullingworth Village Primary School

Flutter, Flutter

Fragile super delicate butterflies.
Always flying around.
Flapping their colourful wings
Never make a sound.

Butterflies sipping from a flower
They always land on something they find.
Fluttering, fluttering about in the sky
They look like they're very kind.

Amna Ali (8)
Cullingworth Village Primary School

Spooky Ghosts Are Coming

Spooky ghosts are coming
And they're going to give you a fright,
Boo! spooky ghosts are coming,
So you better get ready to hide.
They're in your hair,
They're in the air,
So get ready to hide or run.
They are ugly and freaky,
Horrible and scary,
The most important thing is that they are *mean, mean, mean.*

Amy Hanson (9)
Cullingworth Village Primary School

Dolphins

Fantastic dolphins, swimming about.
Graceful and glorious, floating no doubt.
Splashing and shimmering in the water.
Dolphins in the sea.

Abigail Whitehouse (8)
Cullingworth Village Primary School

Splish, Splash, Dolphins

I like dolphins, they're so fun
Wet and shiny and big and blue.

Why don't you come and join our den
Where we come and play our games.

We are good and they are fun
So why don't you be one of us.

Olivia Dalton (8)
Cullingworth Village Primary School

Butterfly

Butterfly, butterfly, fly up high,
You can see all of the open sky.
You flap your wings so beautiful
You fly so high, you never say bye.

Butterfly, butterfly, where do you live?
You can tell me, I won't tell.
You will hide away in your special den
Will you bring me back a shiny shell?

Charis Halliwell (8)
Cullingworth Village Primary School

Dogs

Dogs are furry
They're always out and about
They always want their breakfast

They're funny and silly
And hide, and then you can't find them
It is easy but sometimes it is hard.

Holly Robinson (7)
Cullingworth Village Primary School

The Little Friendly Butterfly

The Little, friendly butterfly
Flying in the air,
She landed on a tree
And started to stare.
The cute, shiny butterfly
But she did not care,
She fell in the pool,
Beautiful butterfly
Flying in the air,
She bumped into a wall
But did not care.

Lucy Riley (8)
Cullingworth Village Primary School

Beautiful Dolphin Poem

Dolphins are blowing through their spouts,
Jumping above the waves so beautiful and proud,
You will find them in the sea and they are lovely to see.
They are delicate
Hopefully they will be saved.

Francesca Haigh (7)
Cullingworth Village Primary School

Dolphins

The beautiful brilliant blue dolphins
Shimmering shivering in the sea
Loving, leaping furious things they can be
Splashing, spattering near the reef
They just want to have some fun and play.

Tasha Smith (8)
Cullingworth Village Primary School

Twinkling Dolphins

Dolphins are dazzling in the open sea,
Dolphins are splattering in the water,
They get very hungry but that makes them stronger,
Dolphins dazzle and sparkle in the sea.

Dolphins are slippery but you can have a stroke,
Dolphins are smooth and soft like a bird,
They try to get your attention,
So that they can play.

Lauren Hawkes (7)
Cullingworth Village Primary School

Birds

The birds glide over the high tide.
The birds swoop down to the bottom of the sea.
The eagles go down on their sides.
On the beach the birds love it.

The geese always rise upon the lovely shore.
On the shore the birds lay and sit.
On the beach the birds love it.

Rhianna Lavery (8)
Cullingworth Village Primary School

Beautiful Dolphin

Dolphins are splashing in the water
Slipping and sliding playing fun games,
They are playing in the sparkling sea.
The dolphins are blazing in the water.
Stars are twinkling on the dolphins,
And the moon shines down on them.

Eve Knowles (7)
Cullingworth Village Primary School

Train

Smoke spitter,
Rail clinger,
Head turner,
Noise maker,
Coal burner,
Rocket sprinter,
Luggage carrier,
Coach marrier,
Station leaper,
Champion puller,
Heavyweight champion,
Kid carrier,
Kettle warmer,
Fast finisher,
Cattle scarer,
Steam hisser,
Olympic racer,
Water guzzler,
Wheel screecher,
Track follower,
Wheel spinner,
Forest traveller,
Head chopper,
Piston pusher,
The train.

Joshua Hardy (10)
Cullingworth Village Primary School

My Grandad

His hair is like a silver blanket, wrapped around the side of his head.
His eyes are like a gleaming porthole to another dimension.
His hands are like moving ice cubes, ready to freeze your cheeks.
His back is like a robot's, slowly and steadily stiffening.
My grandad is a silver blanket, gleaming porthole,
Moving ice cube robot.

Holly Spence (10)
Cullingworth Village Primary School

My Dog

Bird chaser
Garden racer
Stick bringer
Noise ringer

Trouble maker
Morning waker
Firework hater
Dinner waiter
Cuddle giver
That's my favourite dog Buster.

Alex Wright (10)
Cullingworth Village Primary School

King's Slave

What an awful thing
That happened to the king
When his servant died on the floor,
She muttered and whined,
And tutted and cried,
As she died on the king's kitchen floor.

Sarah Bell (11)
Cullingworth Village Primary School

Cars

Slim silver
Glittering sun
Road racer
Sun shiner
Winter loser
Ferrari chaser
Cool colour.

Conor Mayling (11)
Cullingworth Village Primary School

Spring!

The grass is green, the birds can sing,
Oh my gosh it must be spring.
Pink and red flowers,
I could smell them for hours.
The birds in the sky,
Fly so high.
The bumblebee,
Builds its hive, in the tree.
The tree blooming with a rose,
A sweet smell around my nose.
Something's been born, it's a sheep,
It already knows how to leap.
A fluffy white cloud,
Not roaring so loud.
All the animals have a lot of fun,
And they like playing in the sun.

Jenny Makinson (10)
Cullingworth Village Primary School

Kangaroo

Bouncy kangaroos are bouncing
Jumpy kangaroos are jumping
Speedy kangaroos are speeding on the track
Jumping kangaroos are jumping

Bouncy kangaroos are bouncing
Sprinting kangaroos are sprinting
Hurdling kangaroos are hurdling

Lightning kangaroos are lightning
Flash kangaroos are running in a flash
Quick kangaroos are running quickly.

Max Milne (8)
Cullingworth Village Primary School

Seasons

Winter
So cold and frosty in that walk.
Then coming home to a nice warm house.
Feels so nice and cosy.

Spring
Moving on to spring now. Eh!
Seeing new life come into the world.
Feels so lovely to me.

Summer
Summer the warmest time of year.
Feeling the sun on my skin.
Feels so warm and lovely.

Autumn
Leaves are falling to the ground.
Red, yellow and brown.
Feels a colourful time of year.

Julia Proctor (9)
Cullingworth Village Primary School

The Fox!

The cunning sound of the fox will dart around.
The quickness of the fox is very energetic.
And it's soundless when it pounds.
Look out for the fox!

The fox is furry and cleverly skilful.
He is tricky to hunt down because of his speed
But he could kill a furious bull.
Look out for the fox!

The soft skin of the fleece.
The peaceful rushing of his pacing around.
When the hunters come, he wishes he had some peace.
Look out for the fox!

Lewis Whitehouse (8)
Cullingworth Village Primary School

Hippo

Hippos are old and boring,
Ginormous and smelly too,
Steady and slow, lazy and a bit muddy,
Hot and kind of dreary as well.

Now the floor is muddy,
I promised what will happen,
You'll get tired as they're dozing in the sun,
You will not see them having fun.

Rosie Findlay (8)
Cullingworth Village Primary School

Hippo

Hippos swimming through the mud
Smelly things they are
Never touch a bar of soap!

Stupid things they are
Never think of a single thing.
Mean to everything that walks past.

Matthew Wiggins (8)
Cullingworth Village Primary School

Dolphins Gorgeous

Dolphin gorgeous in the dreadful sea.
Upon oceans to see and be
Lovely fishes swimming around
People scared because there's sharks around.
Horses in the sea.
In all the waves,
Nervous people to be afraid!

Aimee Robinson (8)
Cullingworth Village Primary School

Dolphins

D olphins are dripping with crystal-blue water
O ld dolphins are still as acrobatic as they were
L iving under the sea mustn't be easy
P leasing the fishermen must be quite hard
H olding their tail they will take you for a ride
I ncoming dolphins are jumping and singing
N aughty little fish are getting in the way.

Samantha Grimshaw (7)
Cullingworth Village Primary School

Kitty Cat

My kitty is lovely and pretty.
Do you like it?

Cats are very cute and funny creatures.
Do you agree?

Cats like to be playful and steady with kittens.
Are you satisfied?

I like cats do you?

Georgina Dawson (7)
Cullingworth Village Primary School

Slow Tortoises

Tortoises walking slowly.
Hides in its solid shell.
Walking sluggish.
To the juicy bushes.
Tortoise protecting itself from prey.
Rolling side to side.
Trying to get up.
When they roll over.

Callum Whitehouse (8)
Cullingworth Village Primary School

The Sea

The sea is a gigantic barking dog
Waiting for its waves to pounce at the soft wet seashore.
When it's windy, giant tidal waves race down the sea
Like rockets destroying everything in its path.
Lighthouses shake with fear pleading for it to stop.
Thunder and lightning shoots at the sea
As it bashes against the sharp, jagged rocks.
The fish in the sea are petrified by the trembling noises.

Sam Clare (10)
Cullingworth Village Primary School

Tigers Are Terrific

T errifying tigers, tender and terrific.
I nteresting animal in the jungle.
G reat growling, ghostly.
E at anything and explore.
R unning roaring racing.

Jack Griggs (8)
Cullingworth Village Primary School

Elephant

Big elephant, charging down the road.
Swaying head hitting anything that gets in its way.
Charging down like a grey rock.
It's a big thing so watch out or else.
He'll give you a big, big fright!
You'll never be safe.
He'll charge you down like an ant.

Joe Williams (8)
Cullingworth Village Primary School

Hallowe'en

H orrible witches guarding their brooms
A nimals crawling up the side of their hair
L ots of light coming form the pumpkin's eyes
L ittle children running round knocking on doors
O ld women saying go away with anger
W ith big beady eyes, being watched by the skeleton
E ager ghosts looking for their first victim
E nd this party screamed the boggy monster
N ice people giving away sweets.

Tom Williams (9)
Cullingworth Village Primary School

Christmas

C hristmas is a festival in winter
H aving presents means that someone likes you
R eminding people to buy you presents, means that you will get more
I ce is on the ground, when it is Christmas
S now is also on the ground after it has fallen out of the sky
T he amount of presents we get is amazing
M aking snowmen is fun at Christmas
A fter Christmas you get to play with all your toys
S nowball fights happen when the snow falls out of the sky.

Joe Robinson (10)
Cullingworth Village Primary School

Hallowe'en

S weets we all love
C hocolate we eat on that night
A t Hallowe'en we love it
R ocks we crush all day long
Y awn in the morning.

Harrison Bailey (10)
Cullingworth Village Primary School

Dog

Enduring sprinter,
Bone pursuer,
Merciless eater,
Fuss maker,
Food taker,
Sprint maker,
Water spiller,
Boundary maker,
Dog howler,
Sheet ripper,
Smell seeker,
Gobble, gobble,
It's gone.

Sam Ellis (10)
Cullingworth Village Primary School

Car Racer

Wind blower
Car racer

Nitrous zoomer
Sweet spoiler

360 spinner
Extra exhaust

Blinding headlights
Cool doors

Automatic doors
Hydraulics up.

Henry Presland (10)
Cullingworth Village Primary School

What Wayne Became

Isn't it such a shame,
Of what became,
Of Wayne.

Ever since he started school,
He's seemed to be more cool.

He's certainly changed quite a lot,
Since he's been a robot!

Paul Norfolk (10)
Cullingworth Village Primary School

Bedtime

8 o'clock time for bed
You're tired sleepy head.
Sleeping and snoring
In the night
Soon it will be
Daylight.

Sally Handford (10)
Cullingworth Village Primary School

Alien

I am an alien,
I'm here from Mars
And your new world ruler,
I'm green I'm mean and here to stay
I'll exterminate anyone who's in my path
So step down, I'm in charge now!

Ellie Holgate (10)
Cullingworth Village Primary School

My Cat TC

Speeding furball
Leg warmer
Plate liker
Greedy eater
Fridge walker
Animal dustbin
Bird killer
Mouse hunter
Digging digger
Thunder runner
Tail chaser
Cat fitter.

Joe Perrin (10)
Cullingworth Village Primary School

My Dog

Giddy kipper
Animal dustbin
Greedy eater
Flapping wings
Cat lover
Champion racer
Spider destroyer
Tail wager
Leg warmer
Mad machine
That's my best dog Storm.

Alicia Brigg (10)
Cullingworth Village Primary School

My Dog Holly

Shy bundle
Greedy eater
Leg warmer
Dish cleaner
Tea thief
Hugging machine
Barking mad
Flapping wings
Cat hater
Bulldozer
Spider destroyer
Wiggly tail
Terrifying teeth
Mad machine.

Joe Ferguson (10)
Cullingworth Village Primary School

Topsy Turvy Summer

Tune in to your telly
And you will find out
What the real weather
Is in summer,
'Today in summer it will
Be rain in the north
Rain in the south
And rain everywhere else'
The weatherman will say
So find that console
And sit down comfy
Because you will need it today!

Leah Kerr (10)
Cullingworth Village Primary School

Baked Beans

I'm
Yummy, yummy
Mmm, mmm
You'll lick your lips
Because I'm so tasty

I'm
Dressed in sauce
And I'm dancing in flavour

I'm
In a tin
Packed with love
And there are lots of us

So why not go down to the shop
And buy a tin of
Baked beans!

Molly Harrison (10)
Cullingworth Village Primary School

Football

F ootball the players never want to cut the ball.
O ver! shouts the referee when the ball goes over.
O oh goes the crowd when a fowl.
T attoo of England, on the England fans.
B oo! The crowd shouts when a card, card for nothing.
A manager's sad for his team losing.
L ook is frown at the rubbish players.
L ack of spirit when they lose the match.

William Keeley (9)
Cullingworth Village Primary School

Shark

Sharks are vicious
They want something delicious
But they are not delicious.

They jump up high
Like an apple pie
They always tell a lie.

When you are at the surface
With a shark at the surface
Roar.

And after that
When the beach is closed
You need some clothes
And go to 'Dirty Joe's'.

And go to the 'Krusty Crabs'
To buy a 'Krabby paddy'
And feed it to your little laddy.

Luke Crowther (9)
Cullingworth Village Primary School

Hallowe'en Night

Hallowe'en is when werewolves
Prowl and roam the earth at night.
Spiders crawl and ghosts loom
Round every corner shop.
Hallowe'en is what vampires love
It's Hallowe'en night.
Skeletons clink and spirits bang
On Hallowe'en night.

George Trudgill (10)
Cullingworth Village Primary School

A Dolphin's Dream

D elicate as butterflies.
O n and on they swim.
L oving as parents.
P atient as tortoises.
H aving fun with children.
I n the shallow pool.
N udging each other kindly.

D ishes full of fish.
R ainbow fish galore.
E els squirming in the trays.
A rmful of fresh fish.
M ash it all together to make dolphin soup!

Jenny Riley (9)
Cullingworth Village Primary School

Fairies

I really love fairies
They are filled with kindness and love
I don't know if you believe in them or not
They have wings that I've not got.
They always leave a trail of fairy dust
That glitters and twirls around!
When your tooth falls out, the fairies
Come and get it, and they never make a sound.
They like to eat fairy cakes,
And love to have fun!
And like to dance in front of the sun.
I'll tell you a big secret,
Keep it to yourself, and don't tell anyone else . . .
I write to the fairies!

Jessica Cain (9)
Cullingworth Village Primary School

Racing

R is for racing trucks or cars or bikes
A is for agitated, agitated race drivers
C is for *crash*, crashing everywhere
I is for impossible, impossible to finish the race
N is for new, drivers getting new cars
G is for great we won the race. *Great!*

Daniel Ogden (10)
Cullingworth Village Primary School

Rose

R upert is my favourite toy
O range is my favourite fruit
S ummer is the best time of year
E aster is chocolate time.

Samantha Robinson (9)
Cullingworth Village Primary School

Roller Coaster

Going up, going down
Your feet nearly touching the ground
On it you forget how scared you were before
When it's finished
You just want more.

Freya George (10)
Cullingworth Village Primary School

Haiku

I shout as loud as
I can, tig! as I push you,
You fall to the ground.

Edward Donaldson (8)
Dalton Listerdale J&I School

Haiku

Children shouting, stop.
Children playing football games.
People cry I'm hurt.

Bradley Smith (8)
Dalton Listerdale J&I School

Haiku

Children playing tig
Children falling over, 'Ouch'
Getting muddy fast.

Jessica Taylor (8)
Dalton Listerdale J&I School

Haiku

Children playing tig
Children fighting getting hurt
Teachers telling off.

Nula Fell-Andrews (8)
Dalton Listerdale J&I School

Haiku

Conkers falling down.
I have lots of conkers.
Children shouting mine.

Thomas Worrall (8)
Dalton Listerdale J&I School

Haiku

The smell of flowers
I see my friends playing tag
Conkers on the ground.

Nicola Beaumont (8)
Dalton Listerdale J&I School

Haiku

I smell sweet flowers.
Hear people shouting loudly.
Conkers on the ground.

Lauren Carr (8)
Dalton Listerdale J&I School

Haiku

Children arguing
Fighting over the football
Finally friends now.

Sadie Agana (8)
Dalton Listerdale J&I School

Haiku

Children playing tig
Running fast, crashing badly
Getting muddy quick.

Emma Botfield (8)
Dalton Listerdale J&I School

Haiku

I can hear shouting
I'm shouting even louder
But my friend is not.

Ryan Bagnall (8)
Dalton Listerdale J&I School

Haiku

Boys playing football,
Running fast to kick and score.
Shouting, 'Yes, a goal!'

Ashley Wilson (8)
Dalton Listerdale J&I School

Haiku

Children shouting stop.
Do not play football today
'Cos it's not your turn.

Oliver Curran (9)
Dalton Listerdale J&I School

Haiku

I have got the ball
I am running with the ball
I have scored a goal.

Benjamin Malin (8)
Dalton Listerdale J&I School

Haiku

I can see conkers,
Lying on the wet, dark Earth,
Waiting to be picked.

Lucia Del Pozo-Largo (8)
Dalton Listerdale J&I School

Ages

When I was zero I was a hero.
When I was one I had my nappy on.
When I was two I used the loo.
When I was three I hugged a tree.
When I was four I closed the door.
When I was five I saw a beehive.
When I was six I picked up sticks.
When I was seven, by the way I'm Kevin.
When I was eight I sat up straight.
When I was nine I was fine.
When I was ten I was a hen.

Harris Moran (9)
Dodworth St John The Baptist CE (VA) Primary School

Cats And Dogs

My cat Maizy and my dog Millie
Love to play,
Then they will
Attack you
All day.

Madigan Patzelt (9)
Dodworth St John The Baptist CE (VA) Primary School

Games

I like to play games
And I like to win
Having fun with my friends,
Is the best thing.

PS2, Nintendo, it doesn't really matter,
I'll try to beat the high score,
With it, I will shatter.

My little brother
Puts four discs in.
He bends it
And snaps another.

He moans for games to play,
He scratches them,
He breaks them
And buys them another day.

Not only do I like playing games,
I like making them too,
I'll make a character
And it will get you.

I'll make a level
My character explores
He wrecks the place
And now there are falling doors.

How much I like it,
You'll never guess,
If I tell you
You'll be impressed.

Sheldon Delices (8)
Dodworth St John The Baptist CE (VA) Primary School

My Cat And Dog

My dog is silly.
His last name is Billy.
He likes my cat
Who plays with his toy bat.
My cat scratches Jasper on the face.
Then he runs all over the place.
He gets him back
And my mum says he's as black as a sack.
He chases Toby till night
And Toby was so bright.
My cat runs off
And my dog follows him
And that is my story of my dog and cat.

Emma Martin (8)
Dodworth St John The Baptist CE (VA) Primary School

My Dog, My Guinea Pig, My Rabbit

My dog's called Molly, she's really cute and bonny
She likes to play, nearly every day,
She doesn't always get her own way.
She is really pretty
She barks when she spots a kitty.
I love my dog Molly.

My rabbit's called Smudge, my guinea pig's called Fudge.
They like to play, I see them nearly every day.
They like to play in the hay
I love my guinea pig and rabbit.

Hannah Carr (9)
Dodworth St John The Baptist CE (VA) Primary School

My Dog Bell

My dog Bell went for a walk
And fell over a shell
She barked at Mum
And told her off
And she went into the water
And rolled and really smelt.

Tomas Sellars (8)
Dodworth St John The Baptist CE (VA) Primary School

Pets

My pet rabbit Flops is black and white
And she likes to dig all day long.
She rolls in the mud, it makes her smell so bad,
We bring her in at night and give her a bath.

Adelle Wragg (8)
Dodworth St John The Baptist CE (VA) Primary School

At The Zoo

I went to the zoo with a few friends
One of them called Sue
I went round the corner
And I saw a kangaroo.
I went forth and I heard a squawk
I went to see what it was
A parrot that talked.

Imogen Wainwright (8)
Dodworth St John The Baptist CE (VA) Primary School

Animals

The fish wanted to go in the dish.
The shark wanted to go in the park.
The dog wanted to go to the bog.
The cat goes silly over the bat.

Ashley Horsfield (9)
Dodworth St John The Baptist CE (VA) Primary School

It's As Easy As . . .

It's as easy as to drink ink
Or getting a cow to go pink.
It's as easy as going to walk on the planet
Or eating a burger made out of granite.
It's as easy as to give the flower power
Or to climb up a tall tower.
It's as easy as sitting in a fire
Or breathing in a tyre.
It's as easy as riding a duck
Or giving a child a lemon to suck.
It's as easy as cutting your hair
Or cuddling a grizzly bear.
It's as easy as asking a witch to fly with me
Or to fly with a tree.
It's as easy as drinking blood
Or to eat mud.
It's as easy as sitting on a fire
Or to fly higher and higher.
It's as easy as walking on the moon
Or to tell a teacher to turn into a balloon.
It's as easy as seeing a ghost
Or to tell a dog to roast.
It's as easy as seeing a coin talking
Or to see the sun walking.

Naeema Goolab & Saira Mahmood (10)
Field Lane JI&N School

It's As Easy As . . .

It's as easy as making a duck talk
Or asking a crocodile to close his jaws.
It's as easy as sitting in a fire
Or telling a dog to say, 'Sire!'
It's as easy as falling off a tree
Or telling a snail to run free.
It's as easy as flying with a kite
Or telling a planet to look for a site.
It's as easy as flying with a witch
Or making the sun to make a pitch.
It's as easy as burning your face with fire
Or telling a flower to jump.
It's as easy as eating a ball
Or stretching yourself to make you tall.
It's as easy as eating glass
Or running the year 6 class.

Hamzah Laher (10)
Field Lane JI&N School

It's As Easy As . . .

It's as easy as eating a flower
Or getting a big tower.
It's as easy as making a planet walk
Or getting it to talk
It's as easy as flying a white kite
Or holding it tight.
It's as easy as picking your snot
Or getting a new pot.
It's as easy as pawing your hand in the air
Or going to a fair.
It's as easy as looking at the sun
Or eating a big bun.
It's as easy as cutting your hair
Or giving a cuddly bear.

Aysha Hussain (10)
Field Lane JI&N School

The Mighty Aeroplane

It lives in a house,
No way fit for a mouse.
Its home is dark, cold and clean,
It sometimes comes in green.

Its arms are always out,
But they cannot hold.
Its head is fair and bold.
It sings in delight of its ability,
It can hold five hundred people, that's its capability.

It has feet that rotate,
That ascend and descend.
It travels from state to state,
Its nose is large and great.

It has a face of confidence,
But it never moves it,
When it stops, it stops and does not sit
It is the mighty aeroplane,
It is not insane.

Muhammed Talkeen Pandor (11)
Field Lane JI&N School

It's As Easy As . . .

It's as easy as drinking diesel
Or feeding a weasel
It's as easy as licking someone's feet
Or keeping with the beat
It's as easy as telling Mr Patel to leave his job
Or telling Spud to find Bob
It's as easy as looking after sheep
Or going to sleep
It's as easy as burning your house
Or eating a mouse.

Samee Masood (10)
Field Lane JI&N School

The Mean Steal Machine

It roars like a bison
And it looks like my dog Tyson
It eats Daz
And washes my dad's shin pads
It's a devil in Hell
And it loves licking shells
It sticks its arms out
And takes all the clothes for a wash
And does not like people acting posh
It sucks up all the clothes
And it likes people's noses
It licks up all the washing liquid
And it smells like my friend Pikuid
It piles its boogies
And runs like roly poly
It's a very big pest
And it never has a rest

Have you found out what it is?

It's a washing machine.

Tayyub Hussain (10)
Field Lane JI&N School

It's As Easy As . . .

It's as easy as making a tree walk
Or getting a planet to talk.
It's as easy as asking a cow to go on a date
Or telling a baby to climb up a gate.
It's as easy as making a giraffe shrink
Or getting a fly to turn pink.
It's as easy as getting a worm to buy you a car
Or making a dog catch a star.
It's as easy as telling a shark to cook
Or making a worm eat a book.
It's as easy as turning the sun brown
Or making a pear wear a queen's crown.

Aamirah Sidat (10)
Field Lane JI&N School

Friends

Chorus
Field Lane School is a special place
See the smile on our face!
We help and share
At our school everything is fair

We are the best
Better than the rest
Together is better than one
We have so much fun

If you every feel ill
Take the friendship pill
No need for a trial
All you need is a smile

Helping, is what girls do
You can join us girls, too
We love doing each other's hair
Not only that, we always share

That's about us
Don't make a fuss
Well this is where it ends
Wanna be our friend?

Naafiah Loonat, Haarla Sadiq & Ammaarah Pandor (10)
Field Lane JI&N School

It's As Easy As . . .

It's as easy as a snail winning a race
Or telling an ant to pick up a suitcase.
It's as easy as a witch being nice
Or telling a cat to eat some rice.
It's as easy as looking at the sun
Or telling an ogre to have some fun.
It's as easy as telling someone to drink diesel
Or trying to feed a weasel.

Mehran Ishaq (10)
Field Lane JI&N School

Will The Corn Be Ready?

A tractor came and ploughed the field,
And planted corn slow and steady,
The farmer thought about harvest in eight weeks time,
And said, 'Will the corn be ready?'

Emerald shoots grow in the field,
Strawberries become ripe and ready,
It's now six weeks to harvest,
And the corn still isn't ready.

The green corn now is the proper size,
Potato plants are ready,
It's exactly four weeks 'til harvest,
And the corn still isn't ready.

The corn is now golden and ripe,
And in the mills the ovens are ready,
It's now two weeks to harvest,
And hooray the corn is ready.

The farmer looks at his empty field,
Picks up a loaf of bread,
Today's the harvest festival,
Where he gives and shares his bread.

Lizzy Purdy (11)
Garton-on-the-Wolds CE (VC) Primary School

Harvest

Farmers harvesting
Snails crawling
Trees waving
Crops growing
Seeds popping
Strawberries ripening
Thank you for
The harvest.

Johnny Wheatley (10)
Garton-on-the-Wolds CE (VC) Primary School

Harvest

Leaves fall,
Leaves crunch,
They all fall down in a bunch,
Sky's blue,
Grass is green,
Leaves fall on the windscreen.

Tractors plough,
Crops are ripe,
All the way through the night,
Fresh hay,
All day,
Animals, *'Get out the way!'*

This is the way harvest is,
Thank You Lord for sharing it,
We come to church to share our food,
When we're all happy and in the mood.

Abigail Longney (9)
Garton-on-the-Wolds CE (VC) Primary School

Listen To The Sound Of Autumn

Listen to the sound of autumn,
The leaves falling,
Snails crawling.

Listen to the squirrels scampering,
The trees blowing,
And rabbits going.

Listen to the sound of autumn,
Combines working,
Tractors moving.

Listen to the sound of harvest,
Harvest suppers about to start,
Thank You God for our harvest food.

Emily Iveson, Eleanor Lodge & Danielle Wheatley (8)
Garton-on-the-Wolds CE (VC) Primary School

Thanksgiving

Corn churns,
Leaves crunch,
Tractors creak
Haystacks
Birds sing,
Engines roar,
Wind whispers
Crops plenty,
Tractors ploughing
Combines roaring.
Thanksgiving,
To the farmers,
For the harvest of their crops.

James Watts (9)
Garton-on-the-Wolds CE (VC) Primary School

Harvest-Time

Leaves crunching
Leaves falling
Birds singing
Tractors creaking
Snails slithering
Snails crawling
Trees twisting
Combines twirling
Harvest-time.

Chris Fearnley (9)
Garton-on-the-Wolds CE (VC) Primary School

Harvest

Carrots that crunch,
Barley in the fields,
Grapes in a bunch.

Raspberries with pips,
Radishes in the ground,
Potatoes for chips.

Beans in a tin,
Blackberries so juicy,
They run down your chin.

Come and share our harvest,
And give thanks for our crops.

Oliver Noblett (10)
Garton-on-the-Wolds CE (VC) Primary School

Harvest

See the tractors collecting crops
Ready to be sold in the shops

Listen to the boat crackle
As the fisherman fishes for cod and Mackerel

Hear the acorns pop and spark
And there's the children playing in the park

So there's the food coming out of store
Ready to be given to the poor.

Matthew Evans (9)
Garton-on-the-Wolds CE (VC) Primary School

Harvest

Leaves fall,
Snails crawl,
Leaves crunch,
In a bunch,
Crops grow,
In a row,
Trees twist,
In the mist,
Seeds fresh,
They're the best,
Oats so crunchy,
They're so munchy
Thank You Lord for all these things.

Tom Iveson (10)
Garton-on-the-Wolds CE (VC) Primary School

Harvest

Combine harvester cutting the corn
Crops ready for the harvest festival
Come and see our harvest food.

We all gather together
To celebrate in church
We give thanks to God
And share our food with others.

Josh Young & Jake Bowers (9)
Garton-on-the-Wolds CE (VC) Primary School

Seeds

Seeds that twist and blow
Through the wind peacefully
Seeds with long, straight wings
That whirl and twirl around.

Seeds that blow, float and twizzle
Leaves and trees having a dance
The leaves that twirl and whirl
And the thistledown that tickles.

Seeds that burst into plants
Vegetables and fruits that grow
They like the place they grow
They're slow, but they will be pretty.

Seeds with hooks that cling and crunch
Seeds that plant themselves so they can grow
Into a beautiful plant
Then next it will he harvest
Then everything will start again.

Harvey Booth (11)
Garton-on-the-Wolds CE (VC) Primary School

Feelings

As happy as golden sun,
As sad as a dog on a chain,
As calm as the sea,
As scared as a baby on its own,
As angry as a charging bull,
As excited as a clockwork clown.

Victoria Cox (8)
Meadstead Primary School

Feelings

Mad
I feel as mad as the big, steaming red bull.

Happy
I feel as happy as blue rain falling from the sky.

Tired
I feel as tired as a yawning baby.

Shocked
I feel shocked when the lightning strikes.

Calm
I feel as calm as the calm blue sea.

Anxious
I feel as anxious as a fish near a shark.

Sad
I feel as sad as if the world was ending.

Andrew Jessop (9)
Meadstead Primary School

Feelings

Happy as a pink laughing clown,
Sad as a green popped balloon,
Shocked as a goldfish that's been hooked,
Calm as a wave at the blue sea,
Angry as a red bull,
Scared as a white cat up a tree,
Surprised as an awakening black bat,
Excited as a yellow fish being fed.

Patrick Dexter (8)
Meadstead Primary School

Feelings

Sad
I feel as sad as a goldfish in a bowl.

Frustrated
I feel as frustrated as a hamster locked away.

Happy
I feel as happy as the sun rising on the beach.

Angry
I feel as angry as a bull in a tiny pen.

Terrified
I feel as terrified as a horse hanging in a crate
Being moved onto a boat.

Excited
I feel as excited as a cat having a baby kitten.

Surprised
I feel surprised, a present delivered to my door.

Worried
I feel as worried as a cow, being taken away
To a place it is not familiar with.

Helena Quinn (9)
Meadstead Primary School

Feelings

Happy is yellow,
Jealous is gold,
Excited is orange,
Anxious is grey,
Sad is blue,
Frustrated is black,
Mad is red.

Chelsea Levitt (8)
Meadstead Primary School

Wizards

Wizards are funny, wizards are strange
That's how I like it
And it shouldn't change.
Wizards are magic, wizards are magic
They can change like this.
The magic changes in a puff of smoke and a flash of light.

Ethan King (8)
Meadstead Primary School

The Life Of Henry VIII

Since Henry was a boy he was treated very grand,
He loved tennis and music and played well in a band.
When his dad died he became the King,
Six times he wore the wedding ring.
As a King he was very tough,
But never seemed to have enough.
Henry had a vicious face,
So covered himself in silk and lace.

He wanted a wife, to have a boy,
That boy would be his pride and joy,
With the first two wives he had no fun,
'Cause none of them gave him a son.
Next came Jane Seymour, the lucky one,
Who made Henry happy with a son,
But then she got very ill and died,
Henry was so sad, he nearly cried.

He desperately had another two wives,
But they didn't work out and one got the slice!
Henry then found the lady, of Catherine Parr,
The only one that got very far.
She stayed with him, till he died,
The only one that survived.
Jane Seymour's son then took his place,
A weakling with a thin, white face.

Lara Wilson (11)
Melbourne Community Primary School

Henry VIII And His Wives

1509 Henry The Seventh dies,
Off to Heaven the great man flies.
Henry The Eighth starts his reign,
He causes many people lots of pain.

Catherine Of Aragon comes up first,
Her previous marriage makes her cursed.
Henry The Eighth gets really annoyed,
So the long marriage is destroyed.

Anne Boleyn is next in line,
She's already pregnant, so she is fine.
Because she produces a girl, which is bad,
Her head for Henry is to be had.

Jane Seymour should bring some luck,
Edward is born but her life is took.
Hooray, hooray a boy at last,
But his TB death comes extremely fast.

Anne of Cleves - what another wife,
But this one didn't get cut with a knife.
In the end she was divorced,
Do you know why she was forced?

Catherine Howard young and fine,
She was fifth along the line.
Not very long after they were wedded,
Catherine Howard was beheaded.

Catherine Parr she's the last wife,
Because Henry dies, no more life.
Edward The Sixth is king for a bit,
At sixteen he was in the grave pit.

Edward Wilkinson (11) & Matty Jackson (10)
Melbourne Community Primary School

Catherine Parr

Catherine Parr's life began,
In the year of 1512,
She was married to Lord Borough,
When she was in her teens,

Lord Borough died soon after that,
And Catherine married Latimer,
But then he died 15-4-3
King Henry fell in love,

Catherine liked Thomas Seymour,
But married Henry VIII,
For he was the better offer,
She did it for the money,

Henry VIII soon fell ill,
And Catherine had to care for him,
She read to him to go to sleep,
And cared for his three children,

Henry died 15-4-7,
And Catherine was totally free,
She married a man Thomas Seymour,
That same difficult year,

In 1548,
Sadly Catherine died,
She died because of a difficult birth,
And that was Catherine Parr.

Molly Hogan (11) & Megan Lund (10)
Melbourne Community Primary School

Henry VIII

Henry VIII was a funny thing,
He became a great Tudor king,
Many wives he had it was said,
Then it would be, 'Off with her head'
Needing a heir for the throne,
His eyes continued to roam and roam,
Eventually along came Edward, a son!
By now he was all but done.
He got ill and very fat.
In 1547 that was that.
Henry Tudor was dead
Enough said!

Declan Freeman (9)
Melbourne Community Primary School

Flowers

Flowers are sweet
In spring we meet
Buttercups and roses
Tulips make good poses
Flowers need soil and water
Petals can be cut into quarters.
Flowers are *great!*

Megan Wright (8)
Rawmarsh Monkwood Junior School

Roses

Roses are pretty and red and pink, yellow and white.
Our roses, wild roses, does it really matter.
Sun and water is the deal, all food as well.
Eve tho' spring is here, roses are able to be bought in summer.
Spring, summer, each one, it really doesn't matter.

Michaela Richardson (8)
Rawmarsh Monkwood Junior School

Doctor Who

Doctor Who, Doctor Who,
Can I come travelling with you,
Time and space I think it's ace,

We meet aliens and new friends,
Until the invasion ends.

Doctor Who, Doctor Who,
Can I come travelling with you,
Time and space I think it's ace.

Platform One was freaky
Daleks are really sneaky.
We went to Van Staten's lair
It gave us quite a scare.

Doctor Who, Doctor Who
Can I come travelling with you
Time and space I think it's ace.

Cassandra is all skin, that is really thin
Aliens are a really big shock.
So is Jackie, when she's in a frock.

Doctor Who, Doctor Who
Can I come travelling with you.
Time and space I think it's ace.

Megan Scott & Alice Bragg (8)
Rawmarsh Monkwood Junior School

Fairies

Fairies flying in the sky,
Flapping their delicate wings,
You can see their fairy dust,
On a dark, gloomy night.
Fairies are very shy.
They wear pink in the sky,
The tooth fairy comes at night,
And builds a tower with teeth,
At night the queen fairy comes
To have fun at a disco.

Isobel Gough & Carly Jones (8)
Rawmarsh Monkwood Junior School

Football

The players go into the changing room
And the manager says, 'If you don't play good,
You'll be back in the changing room.'
The teams start to play and they get under way.
The Away team scores a goal,
So the manager substitutes Ashley Cole.
Then the home team scores a goal and the crowd roars
Then the Away team are on a roll.

Bradley Hammond & Connor Spyve (8)
Rawmarsh Monkwood Junior School

Roses

Roses, roses shining bright in the sunlight.
How I wish I was you.
Roses, roses shining bright,
Sparkling dew drops on your petals glisten, like a thousand jewels.
How I wish I was you.
Roses, roses shining bright in the pale moonlight
How I wish I was you.

Anna Rodgers (8)
Rawmarsh Monkwood Junior School

Dragons

The big red dragon is fierce and strong,
He lives in a big dark cave
The village people are afraid of him.

A charming knight comes along one day,
The villagers ask him for help.
He rides towards the big, dark cave
And calls the dragon out.

With fiery breath, the dragon roars,
And challenges the charming knight.
With a thrust of his sword, the dragon dies
The villagers cry in delight.

Elisha Ingleby (8)
Rawmarsh Monkwood Junior School

Spaghetti

It's long and thin and I like to suck it in
Spaghetti.
Tomato sauce, thick and red, dribbles down my chin
Spaghetti.
I eat it when I'm in my bed and now it's dribbling down my head
Spaghetti.
When I'm in school, it's really cool to eat
Spaghetti.

Claire Hobson & Bethany Hague (8)
Rawmarsh Monkwood Junior School

Reptiles

Crocodiles are cool, they like swimming in a pool.
Snakes are long and thin and slender,
They'd make a nice bag for my aunt Brenda.
Alligators in the swamp, looking like a big tree log.
Slowly swimming in the water,
Doing what they shouldn't ought to do.
Geckos running up a tree
Doing somersaults so we can see.
I don't think the mighty triceratops
Would be any good at playing hop-scotch.
But best of all the velociraptor,
They really have a very high kill factor.

Liam Larkin & Alex Fields (8)
Rawmarsh Monkwood Junior School

Spider-Man

Spider-Man climbs a wall
Spins his web then jumps.
Spider-Man is big and strong
And fights his enemies all day long.
Spider-Man saves the day
When his enemies come out to play.

Lisa Kelsall & Dylan Robinson (8)
Rawmarsh Monkwood Junior School

London Zoo

London Zoo is a fantastic place to go
Because it has got lots of wild animals
And it is brilliant!

They have hairy gorillas
With a huge, fat bum as big as a rocket
And they are huge!

Zebras are very stripy, as stripy as a painting
With a long tail as an aeroplane and an aeroplane is really long!

There is a Bug World
There are large snails as big as a football!
They make huge snail tracks and they are horrible!

The cheetahs are very good hunters
And they eat buffalos and Warthogs
And they eat them for their *dinner!*

The camels chew horribly and they stink
Because they don't have a bath!

London Zoo have wild hunting dogs!
They have black and white patches on their fur
And they are really good hunters
That's why they're called wild hunting dogs!
They hunt in packs and they have got really sharp teeth.
As sharp as a thorn and they *hurt!*

London Zoo have really big pigs
Almost bigger than my brother!
They have pink and black spots
Because they're different than normal pigs
Because they are wild pigs
And they have curly tails
And they still have piglets and triplets
And they have big snouts.

They have poisonous frogs
With all different coloured ones and different sorts of frogs.

Calum Ward (9)
St Andrew's CE Primary School, Hull

Hull Fair

Glittering big wheel,
Stand to attention.
Waiting for every body to climb on
Slowly going round and round.

Cheeky George tries to
Snatch money from one
As they go past,
George is a hairy gorilla.

Toffee apples covered
In chocolate and hundreds and thousands.
Burgers smelling freshly cooked,
Tasting so delicious.

Beautiful light shines in the pitch-black sky,
The big, bright light scattered all over Hull Fair.
Time goes fast,
Wait for another year.

Courtney Clark (8)
St Andrew's CE Primary School, Hull

Wolves

Strong like a gigantic boulder,
Vicious and looking for tasty blood,
Looking for lovely meat,
Howling loudly at the huge moon
Hunt in fierce packs,
Hairy like a gorilla
There are about twenty types of fierce kinds,
Live in deep and dark forests and rocky mountains,
They drink lovely water,
They hunt in the dark night,
They can smell from a huge distance,
They have some fast movements like a gorilla,
They have some slow movements like a tortoise.

Jay Farrow (8)
St Andrew's CE Primary School, Hull

The Witch's Brew

Into my pot,
There now must go
Two frog's legs
And a pigs little toe,
A tail of a mouse
And a spoonful of fear,
One jug of water and a plateful of keys.
Finally now I can sit down
And have a lovely cup of tea,
I have asked my toad to sit with me,
Sitting with my toad
It said to me,
'You are a witch and you must be a little tiny dragon
With a little dragon attitude'
So now you know what on Earth I mean,
So then I say to my cheeky little pet, that,
'You are such a funny little toad.'

Jadzia Johnson (8)
St Andrew's CE Primary School, Hull

The Explosion In The Toffee Factory

The deranged manager stands around
With brown, sticky toffee in his hair,
His smart workers come in and say, 'I like your hair,'
The manager stares and the workers glare,
Toffee machines explode,
This blissful manager said, 'I like your hair lots today.'
The demented workers scream and shout,
And the manager said, 'What are you lot moaning about?'
Well we're covered in brown, sticky mush . . .
You could be more fond of yourself,
Because you look more peculiar than you used to be . . . !

Banu Senol (8)
St Andrew's CE Primary School, Hull

Candyland

A dazzling chocolate fountain,
With chewing gum galore,
Houses made of candyfloss,
And liquorice on the door,
Sprinkles fall down from the sky,
Pools filled with chocolate sauce,
People made of gingerbread,
Toys made of brandy snaps,
The sun is like a fairy bun,
Gardens grow with chewing gum,
Shops made of minty rock,
Dazzling colours fill the streets,
Trees made of cocoa beans,
On the night, the lights are like a pretty rainbow,
Candyland is an amazing place with lots of secrets hiding around.

Rachel Smith (9)
St Andrew's CE Primary School, Hull

Hull Fair

Hull Fair is the best fair in the whole country.
The delicious smell drifts up your nostrils.
As you stand at the creaky gate.
The huge wagon wheel guarding the enormous
Wonderful Hull Fair.
Fantastic rides with dazzling lights and deafening music.
Mouth-watering hotdogs and juicy burgers.
Pink, fluffy sheep's wool on a long, long, long wooden stick
And hard crunchy brandy snaps.

Luke Brady (8)
St Andrew's CE Primary School, Hull

Candyland

A dazzling chocolate fountain,
With chewing gum galore.
And houses made from candyfloss,
And liquorice on the door,
The moon is like a Hallowe'en treat,
And the sun is like a fairy bun,
Sprinkles fall down from the sky, covering the street,
Pools are filled with chocolate sauce,
And lollipops for the slides,
People are made from gingerbread,
Gardens grow with some lovely sweets,
Trees made of lollipops,
And flowers made from sweets,
Ornaments made from hard stiff rock,
And shops are made from blueberry pie,
And on the night when the liquorice sky turns black,
Amazing colours fill the streets,
Candyland is a dazzling place,
Full of surprises and secrets.

Natasha Barker (8)
St Andrew's CE Primary School, Hull

Wolves

Deer hunter
Buffalo killer
Human eater
Forest dweller
Tunnel digger
Night forager
Grey predator.

Rhys King (8)
St Andrew's CE Primary School, Hull

Seasonal Dragons

Have you heard of the Crystal Snow dragon?
Her skin is as white as snow, she has sky-blue scales,
She breathes pure ice.
She's friends with Crystal Snow fairy,
She hates Jack Frost and his beastly ways,
Even though he makes snow all day,
She lives in a castle, that never melts,
Winter is over now!

Have you heard of Amber Spring dragon?
She has rose, pink skin and orange scales.
She is friends with Tiffany Topaz fairy,
She lives in Topaz Castle,
She breathes acid and poison
Spring is over now!

You must know Scarlet Summer dragon!
She has sunny yellow skin and green scales,
She breathes scolding, blazing, hot fire!
She lives on Sunny Hill,
She is friends with Goldie Sunshine fairy,
She loves to sit on the beach.

Have you heard of Rouge Autumn dragon,
She has red skin and flame-orange scales,
She is friends with Ruby the red fairy,
She lives in Autumn Castle
It's raving,

Now you know about seasonal dragons,
You can tell your friends.
If I told you everything, I'd be here forever!

Shanice Michaels (9)
St Andrew's CE Primary School, Hull

Hull Fair

Hull Fair is the best,
Under the huge, warm tent is filled with entertainment,
Loud noisy music, as loud as a jet.
Loud noises, louder than an air horn,
Food is tasty and mouth-watering,
Amazing rides, as fast as a Grand Prix motorbike,
It's got the best rides and the biggest fair ever,
Rides make your face go white, like snow,
It is so good, people come from all over the world,
Slingshot as dangerous as a bomb attached to you,
All rides as fun as playing with your friends,
Monster House as scary as the Vikings,
Arcade as small as a mouse.
Zooming slingshot quickly goes up and down,
I think next year it will be even better.
Next, it will be even better than this year,
Girls and boys will scream even louder.

Sam Stevenson (8)
St Andrew's CE Primary School, Hull

Witches' Rhyme

We are the witches of Boston Spa
Those who meet come from afar,
We cast our spells
On things foretell
And prefer our broomsticks to a car.

We are the witches of Collingham Wood
Our favourite food is 'toadstool pud'
We drink our brews
Make hedgehog stews
And on special days, drink pints of blood.

Megan Murphy (8)
St Mary's CE Primary School, Wetherby

Conkers

Clang! Clang!
Bash! Bash!
There goes the conkers.
Hear them *clash*
And hear them *bang*.
Quick! Cover your ears.
Children playing.
I win! I win!
That's what you hear
When conkers are about.

Alice Whitelam (8)
St Mary's CE Primary School, Wetherby

My Puppy Dollie

Dark-brown eyes and a cold, wet nose,
Looking for mischief wherever she goes,
Always giddy, ready to play.
My puppy Dollie, brightens my day.

Ruby Barrett (8)
St Mary's CE Primary School, Wetherby

Hallowe'en

The most terrifying things come out and play
Ghosts and ghouls do frightening things, I say,
But will they come and knock on your door,
On this scary day.

Roxanne Frost (10)
St Mary's CE Primary School, Wetherby

Me

My name is Barnaby and I am nine.
I love my parents and my sister's just fine.
Here are some things I love to do
Read along and I'll share with you.
I like to read all my books
I love to play on my new X-Box.
I like to watch the wrestling
Especially when they're in the ring.
Sometimes I swim in my pool,
I love to splash - it's really cool.
You should see me on my chopper,
It's big and red, what a whopper.
I love my life, it's such a joy.
I really am a lucky boy.

Barnaby Peech (9)
St Thomas More Primary School, Sheffield

Autumn, Autumn, Autumn

The summer's gone and autumn is here
The rain pours like a giant waterfall in the sky
The leaves blow like birds in a hurry
The wind blows like the speed of light.

I can smell the leaves decaying in the air
I can hear leaves crunching with every footstep
I can see leaves floating in the breeze
I can feel the wind turning my hands into ice blocks.

Christmas is just a jingle away.

Jade Fletcher (10)
St Thomas More Primary School, Sheffield

Amazing Autumn

The summer's gone, autumn's near.
The strong breeze blows beautifully.
Crunchy conkers crack open.

The sky is grey and dull.
Rain falls like a shower
Leaves fall like flying feathers.

Heavy rain splatters on the ground.
Crispy leaves splitter and splatter
Soggy grass is on your shoes.

Rainy storms come in autumn
It starts to get chilly and chilly.
Blowing branches, blow beautifully
Autumn is amazing.

Olivia Lomas (8)
St Thomas More Primary School, Sheffield

Pegasus

A sparkling flying horse, soaring through the air.
It's a Pegasus!
The sparkly creature has wings, flapping like flames.
He has a tail, flaming behind him.
As soon as the Pegasus, passes the night,
Time starts, his silky, fur shines.

He's like a unicorn, with no horn.
However, the non-magical horse, is handsome and brave.
As he flies, the poet continues to write,

How, in the poet's mind, the Pegasus,
Sparkles and sways.
But the poet has finished, the Pegasus, has gone.
The poem must end, Pegasus does not exist!

Charlotte Betts (8)
St Thomas More Primary School, Sheffield

Autumn

Autumn is a time to play
In the leaves that look like hay!
In the trees that look bare
Autumn time is here.

Autumn is a time where
It is damp, so stamp on summer
Autumn is here.

Autumn is a time with a frosty smell,
Birds singing and cars zooming
So ring that bell and jump to Mars
Autumn time is here.

Autumn is a time when conkers fall
It's a good time to play with a ball
So get down, and shout
Autumn time is here.

Grant Williams (9)
St Thomas More Primary School, Sheffield

Autumn

Autumn, autumn, it's finally here
But watch out because winter's near!
The rain showers down, like tears so light
But the sun comes out, ever so bright.

Hey watch out for those conkers
'Cause if you're not careful they'll drive you bonkers!
Crispy crackly leaves, fall off the trees
Damp, soggy moss all over the place.

The leaves are like golden-brown biscuits.
Outside you can hear the rain on your windows.
Blustery weather can make you shiver
But don't get down because winter's near!

Frances Hemingway (8)
St Thomas More Primary School, Sheffield

Autumn

The autumn has come,
The crispy leaves are here
We feel the breeze at night,
And see the twirly trees.

The rain comes down like
On a child's face like tears
We see the breezy grass
But what about the grasshoppers.

The clouds are black,
It's going to rain
We all need to get in.

It is getting chilly
The leaves are flowing,
They are blowing in your face.
'But Christmas is here!'

Lauren Hodkin (10)
St Thomas More Primary School, Sheffield

Autumn

In the autumn you're bound to see scurrying squirrels
If you're lucky you might get muddy grass
In the autumn, the weather is damp, soggy and chilly
If you go out you need to put your wellies on!

If you stand on a leaf, *crunch, crunch*, that's what you'll hear
The trees sway from side to side
You'll feel cold, so get wrapped up
Autumn is like summer and winter put together.

Natasha Doyle (9)
St Thomas More Primary School, Sheffield

Autumn Sounds

Leaves, leaves golden brown and bronze
Fallen tree branches
Blown off by the current
Of the wind.

Dancing seagulls
Flying in the mist
The crows in their nests
In a tree.

Conkers as loud
As a baby's cry
The ice-cold snow
Up to my knees.

Out in the countryside
Seeing the bees
Collecting their honey and
Jars that smell like roses.

Kayleigh Evelyn (9)
St Thomas More Primary School, Sheffield

My Little Pegasus

One day I was walking through some flowers in a field
And then I saw a lovely Pegasus laying down on her side.
She was sweet and calm
But I haven't told you yet, what colour she was
She was purple and had a wavy mane.
She had curled hair and it was purple
She had a little crown round her head
Everything was purple
She was wonderful and magical.

Bethany Smedley (8)
St Thomas More Primary School, Sheffield

Autumn

When autumn comes and summer goes
Everything feels wet and soggy,
When the rain falls and hits the ground
It sounds like beads falling.

Whether I'm walking or running
I can hear the leaves crunching all around me,
All I taste is coldness
Wrapped around my tongue.

The leaves on the ground are so crunchy
McCoy's yellow crisps,
Now all I hear is the *spps*
Of daddy-long-legs.

Come on autumn's here, let's play,
Let's play all day, *shuush*,
Is that Santa's bells I can hear.

Lauren Raynor-Bennett (9)
St Thomas More Primary School, Sheffield

Angel Fish

An angel fish swam by
And told a big lie
He had a rest
Wearing a blue vest

One angel fish fell from the sky
Up, up, up high
Which made a big splash
And I gave him the cash.

Hannah Stocks (9)
St Thomas More Primary School, Sheffield

I Don't Know What To Call It

When I ate some cake
I began to bake
So I said, 'No, please
Don't put me in the cheese!'

Don't put me with the bees
Nor in the cheese
So cool me down
Don't you frown.

I want to go to school
I won't take a mule
I don't want to do RE
But please let me do PE.

I want to learn about Vikings
I don't want to meet any other kings
So please don't frown
When you cool me down.

Brendan Maycock (8)
St Thomas More Primary School, Sheffield

Autumn

Summer's gone, autumn's here.
It is very damp like slush.
It is very cold and wet,
The leaves are old and brown.

The ground is wet and soggy,
The winter drifts is in the air.
The conkers are as hard as rocks,
As the cold breezes around me.

Alex Radford (9)
St Thomas More Primary School, Sheffield

Autumn

The summer's gone and autumn's here.
Leaves are blowing in the cold breeze
Noisy children playing conkers
Freezing breeze blowing you away.

Look at the rain falling from the sky
Like a winter fountain as birds fly by.
The leaves are blowing by,
Like birds in a fight.

I can see puddles on the ground
I can smell horrid leaves from the trees
I can hear rain falling from the sky
I can feel coldness in my feet
I can taste rain from the clouds.

Grace Swift (9)
St Thomas More Primary School, Sheffield

Autumn

Autumn's here, when summer's gone
Crispy leaves start to appear
Like Walkers crisps scattered around
Up and down the wind shall go
With soaked leaves whirling around.

Amazing apples hanging on the tree
Conkers falling on top of me
Rustly trees acting chilly
I won't do that, because that's
Just silly.

Briony Colton (9)
St Thomas More Primary School, Sheffield

Autumn Poem

Summer's nearly ended, and autumn's near.
The brown leaves on the ground are like brownies.
Autumn is cold, even ice-cold.
The rain is cold, like Antarctica.
In autumn it is so blustery
It blows the leaves around like a hurricane
And there are lightning storms, like soggy puddles.
I can hear crunching leaves.
I can smell decaying leaves.
I can see twinkling stars in the sky.
I can feel the strong breeze all around me.
I can hear strong rain all around me.

Levi Brock (8)
St Thomas More Primary School, Sheffield

Autumn

Christmas comes twice a day
Come on kids it's time to play
Because autumn's here,
Let's play in the leaves today.

Now it's damp it's time to run and stamp.
You hear birds singing every day
So come on kids, let's play, play, play.

Leaves fall like waves in the sea.
Shiny hard, brown leaves falling
Off the tree!

Joe Talbot (9)
St Thomas More Primary School, Sheffield

My Dream Horse

My dream horse is called Candy Love
Her ears stick up like lollipop sticks
Her long mane looks like sweety-red laces
And her lips look shiny like cherry lips
Her body looks like a sugar cube
Her eyes look like white fresh mints
Those beautiful legs look like sticks of rock
Those round hooves look like sugar almonds
Her nose looks like Cola bottles
Her mane drifts in the wind
Her hooves sound like peanuts dropping
Her reins look like rhubarb and custard
That's why I call her Candy Love!

Paris Thorpe (9)
St Thomas More Primary School, Sheffield

Autumn's Here

The summer's gone and autumn's here
Showers from a bottle
The leaves are as colourful as gold
And the trees are like statues

Look at the sparkly drained grass
And the leaves floating from the sky
With the prickly, prickly conkers
But don't be down because Christmas is near.

James Killeen (8)
St Thomas More Primary School, Sheffield

My Auntie

I have an auntie
Her name is Dawn
Soon in November
Her baby will be born.

Soon my auntie
Will be a mummy
I'll buy the baby
A nice Pooh Bear dummy.

My auntie's baby
Makes me happy
But the thing I don't like
Is one stinky nappy!

Hollie Roberts (8)
St Thomas More Primary School, Sheffield

Autumn

The summer's gone and autumn's here.
They're rainy showers and twirly trees.
Watch out for the leaves blowing, like birds in a hurry
The sky is as grey as a pigeon flying in the sky.

All I smell is leaves on the hard bumpy ground.
Crunchy conkers grow on the trees
Watch them go fast.
When you walk, all you hear is *crunch! crunch*!
As you walk on the leaves.

Don't give up, you will not be sad
Because it is autumn
Because Hallowe'en and Christmas are a jingle away.

Catherine Dwaine (8)
St Thomas More Primary School, Sheffield

Autumn

Wind and leaves are blowing around
Ice cold rain and falling conkers
They are like crunchy bars crackling on the floor.

Summer's gone and autumn's here
We're all cold as the strong breeze comes
We're all coming in as the wind's howling
And watching TV or on games.

But Christmas is waiting as autumn ends
We're all waiting for Christmas too
We want to make snowballs and snowmen
But we should be careful we don't want to get a cold.

Adam Cohen (9)
St Thomas More Primary School, Sheffield

Autumn

Autumn's here now
It's freezing cold
The leaves are brown
And you can see daddy-long-legs!

The rain falls like a waterfall
And the leaves are like Walkers crisps,
You can hear the crunchy leaves as
You walk on the path and all the leaves rustling.

You can hear the whistling wind
And the crunchy leaves too
And you can see rain bouncing on your head
And you can taste apples in your mouth.

Olivia Nicholson (9)
St Thomas More Primary School, Sheffield

Excited

It's like getting new teddies
It's like butterflies in your belly
It's like waiting to go and skate
It's like going on a date
It's like buying new clothes
It's like getting ready to pose
It's like getting a horse
It's like waiting to go on a fun course.

Rebecca White (10)
Serlby Park School

Red

It's like a raging fury,
It's like an angry story,
It's like a blazing fire,
It will burn through a tyre,
It's like an angry bull,
It'll rip off your arms and pull,
It's like waiting in a queue,
Waiting to see Man U.

Daniel Hawley (11)
Serlby Park School

Blue

It's like bad weather,
It's like a blue feather,
It's like the clear, crystal sea,
It's like a blue key,
It's like men in blue,
It's like a fountain pen too,
It's like the sky,
It's like a car speeding by
It's like blue!

Kimberley Smith (10)
Serlby Park School

Red

It's like the red glow in a fire,
It's like red flames getting higher and higher.
It's like the red blood vessels rushing through our body,
It's like the red car that belongs to Noddy.
It's like the sky at night,
It's like blood that gives people a fright.
It's like the red shimmer in the sun,
It's like the red icing on top of a bun.
It's like the red pencil pot on the table,
It's like the electricity running through a cable.
It's like a red fog in the sky,
It's like a red parrot flying by.

Sophie Cave (10)
Serlby Park School

Disappointment

It's like not getting any presents.
It's like not being allowed any pets.
It's like not getting any new shoes.
It's like not being allowed any new clothes.

It's like trying your best but never succeeding.
It's like losing your favourite teddy.
It's like planning a perfect picnic and it rains.
It's like breaking your leg, the day before you go on holiday.

Eily Wilson (11)
Serlby Park School

Red

It's like a devil getting mad.
It's like a motorbike, speeding bad.
It's like the strip of Man U.
It's like waiting impatiently in a queue.
It's red, red, it's red.

Makenzie Tomlinson (10)
Serlby Park School

It's Like What Colour?

It's like the sky at sunset
It's like having a pig as a pet
It's like making the boys wink
It's like pink!

It's like a Man U shirt
It's like a colour when you're hurt
It's like your head when you're embarrassed
It's like red!

It's like the sun
It's like the colour of fun
It's like a coloured weird-haired fellow
It's like yellow!

Kelly Smith (10)
Serlby Park School

Red

It's like a blazing fire
Or a skidding tyre
It's like a flame
Or burning shame
It's hot
It comes out with one, single bullet shot
It's red, it's red, it's burning red.

Dale Sawyer (10)
Serlby Park School

Red

It's like the sunset in the sky
It's like a sports car zooming by
It's like a devil in the sky
It's like the hot sun burning in the sky
It's red, it's red, it's burning red.

Ryan Day (10)
Serlby Park School

Angry

It's like the colour red.
It's like the cover on my bed.
It's like red mist in front of my eye.
It's like not succeeding no matter how much you try.
It's like the thunder in the sky.
It's like a vulture flying by.
It's like a bull in a field.
It's like a knight with his shield.

Jake Renshaw (11)
Serlby Park School

How I Feel

It's like when I am down I feel sad,
It's like I am going to get really mad.
It's like when I calm myself down,
It's like I am just a pathetic clown.
It's like trying to make myself happy,
It's like all of my emotions have gone sappy.
My feelings go all over,
Sometimes I am happy, then I am sad.

Shannon O'Hara (10)
Serlby Park School

Sparkling Red

It is like the sky at night, giving shepherd's delight,
It is like the sky in the morning, shepherd's warning,
It is like a fire burning bright,
Sometimes people like the sight.

Fierce and bright,
Sparking and light,
Burning and hot
In a sparky pot.

Amy Ellis & Chloe Lukey (10)
Serlby Park School

Autumn Leaves

Crunchy golden leaves, falling from the trees
In the cool, autumn breeze.
In the park piles of red, brown, yellow and golden
Leaves from the freezing tall trees.
In the sky there are leaves floating from the trees in the breeze
Cornflake noises when the squirrels are running
Through the leaves, finding acorns.

Tia Morris (7)
Serlby Park School

Autumn Leaves

Crumbling leaves start tumbling down,
Red, yellow, orange and golden-brown falling down.
Crunching, crackling cornflakes sound like leaves in the breeze,
In the park where it's dark, the leaves
Start to crunch where the people walk.
The squirrels scram through the leaves looking for acorns.

Paige O'Keeffe (7)
Serlby Park School

Bored

It's like a pen without paper
It's like a board without a pen
It's like a band without a microphone
It's like a singer using the wrong tone.

Connor McGowan (10)
Serlby Park School

Purple

It's like a purple car going fast.
It's like a purple sky shining bright.
It's like a purple hat flowing around in the sea.
It's like a purple zoo turning in purple.
It's like a purple kite flying in the sky.
It's like a purple car driving around.
It's like a purple van going round and round.

Jasmine Spowart (10)
Serlby Park School

The Colour Red

It's like a bunch of roses on Valentine's Day,
It's like a sparkly ruby on a ring,
It's like the colour of poppies on Remembrance Day,
It's like the colour of blood when you bleed,
It's like the colour of the classroom seats we sit on,
It's like a fire burning bright,
It's like the colour of the sky at night,
It's like an England shirt,
It's like some flowers that come in spring.

Chelsea Peace (10)
Serlby Park School

Black

It's like the darkest colour
It's like it couldn't get any duller
It's like darkness at night
It's like far from bright
It's like super dark
It's like as scary as a shark!

Glenn Malkin (11), Jeren Bridgett & Devon Brammer (10)
Serlby Park School

Red

It's like a red hot day.
It's like a sunrise.
It's like a red car passing by.
It's like a red hot chick.
It's like a red-ruby ring.
It's like blood at night.
It's like strawberry jam.
It's like a volcano erupting.
It's like your mother getting angry.
It's like a devil's fire.
It's like a red hot chilli pepper.
It's like a red hot fire at Christmas night.

Luke Butters & Lewis Coxon (10)
Serlby Park School

Blue

It's like an ocean glistening in the night.
It's like being alone in an empty room.
It's like a sky looking into someone's eyes.
It's like the sea glowing in the night.
It's like a sky, it's like a flame of fire.

Charlie Arnott (10)
Serlby Park School

The Colour Red

It's like a rose on Valentine's Day.
It's like some flowers that come in May,
It's like a shining ruby on a ring,
It's like your cheeks glowing when you sing,
It's like the colour on a flag,
It's like some colours on a mag.

Emma Hay (10) & Sarah Taylor (11)
Serlby Park School

Calm

It's like the water passing by,
It's like the sky so high,
It's like the pebbles on a sandy beach,
It's like a rainbow within your reach.

Robyn Hanley (10)
Serlby Park School

The Four Seasons

What is spring?
Birds singing in their nests,
Chicks hatching out of eggs,
Flowers blooming all around,
Everything's peaceful on the ground.

What is summer?
Long afternoons outside,
Playing with my friends for a long time,
Barbecues, ice cream, playing with Sue,
Can't stay writing, lots to do.

What is autumn?
The leaves are falling off the trees,
Everything's dying there's a breeze,
The rain falls heavily down,
The Hallowe'en scares, have come to town.

What is winter?
Winter's here, look at the lights,
Christmas joys, snow and ice,
Playing with snow, playing with presents,
The lights still glow on our crescent.

Megan Wilson (10)
Treeton CE Primary School

A Poem Of Sport

Football, football, football is great,
You can play it with a mate.

Rugby, rugby, rugby is tough,
And can be very rough.

Cricket, cricket, cricket is neat,
Just make sure the others don't cheat.

Tennis, tennis, tennis is chillin',
We can play it if you're willin'.

Golf, golf, golf is cool,
But make sure you know the rule.

Swimming, swimming, swimming is sound,
Just be careful not to drown.

Sport, sport, sport is easily the best,
If I can do it so can the rest!

Josh Pierpoint (10)
Treeton CE Primary School

Long John Silver

I am a splendid cook,
But I am a nasty crook,
I could steal your treasure!
I would do it with pleasure,
I have a wooden crutch,
But it doesn't bother me much!
Because I have a nasty old crew,
If they're good, I'll treat 'em with some brew!
I have a parrot who screeches,
And he copies all my speeches!
For I am Long John Silver, the captain of the sea,
So don't bother messing with me!

Adam Walton (10)
Treeton CE Primary School

The Farmer Poem

Boggis, Bunce and Bean,
One fat, one short, one lean
Those horrible crooks,
So different in looks
Were none-the-less
Equally mean

They're mean to the foxes
Who live in their boxes
So different to be
Between you and me
Those poor, old shy little foxes

But just then one day
The farmers will say
The foxes are sneaky
And incredibly freaky
That they'll just have to pay.

Bethany Farmer (10)
Treeton CE Primary School

Winter

Winter is a season
It snows at winter
The snow crystals fall
It touches me then disappears
It is cold and wet
A silent, white carpet
Covers the rooftops
It covers the trees like tinsel
People trying to walk
Cars trying to drive
But that's what I call *winter*.

Natalie Shawcroft (10)
Treeton CE Primary School

Summer

Summer is here
Hooray for us, it's time
To go and play in the sun.

Over the hills and
Through the countryside
Driving carefully to the seaside.

Waves crashing, sun blazing
Making sandcastles
Playing cheerfully.

It's time to leave and say goodbye
Back through the countryside,
Home we arrive.

Amy Burton (10)
Treeton CE Primary School

A Lion

A lion is so fierce,
And when it bites it will get you,
A horrible bite on your arm or leg,
If you tease it, it will run after you,
All the way home.

So you better keep away from a fierce lion,
One day a lion will get killed by a man,
And then a lion will kill you.

Mica Leaning (10)
Treeton CE Primary School

Summer Sun

When the sun rises,
It warms up the earth,
Its golden rays
Beam down below

Perched up high,
Like a God on His throne
He smiles down on us

As the sun sets over the sea,
People say goodbye,
So tidaldie.

Matthew Badger (10)
Treeton CE Primary School